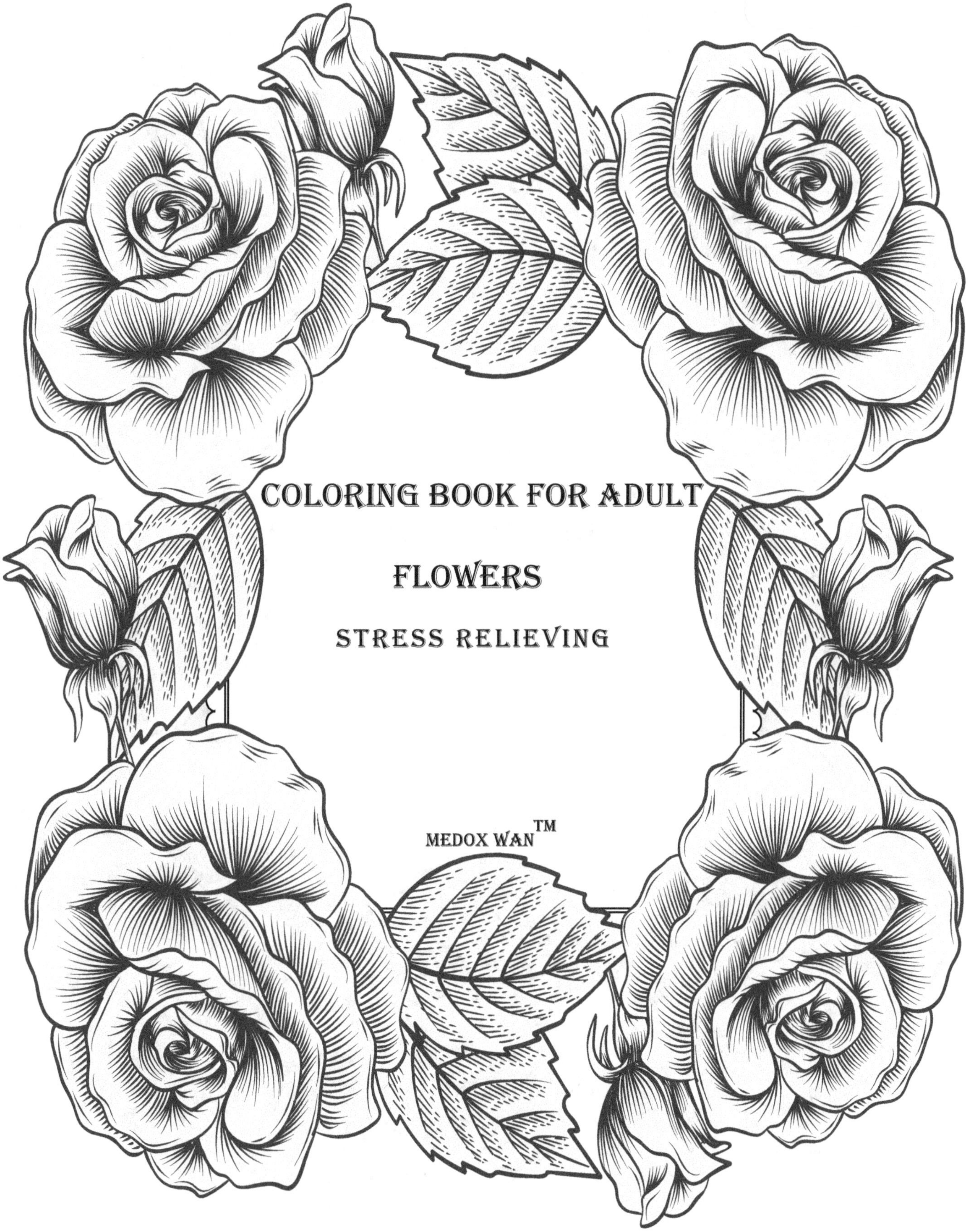

COLORING BOOK FOR ADULT

FLOWERS

STRESS RELIEVING

MEDOX WAN™

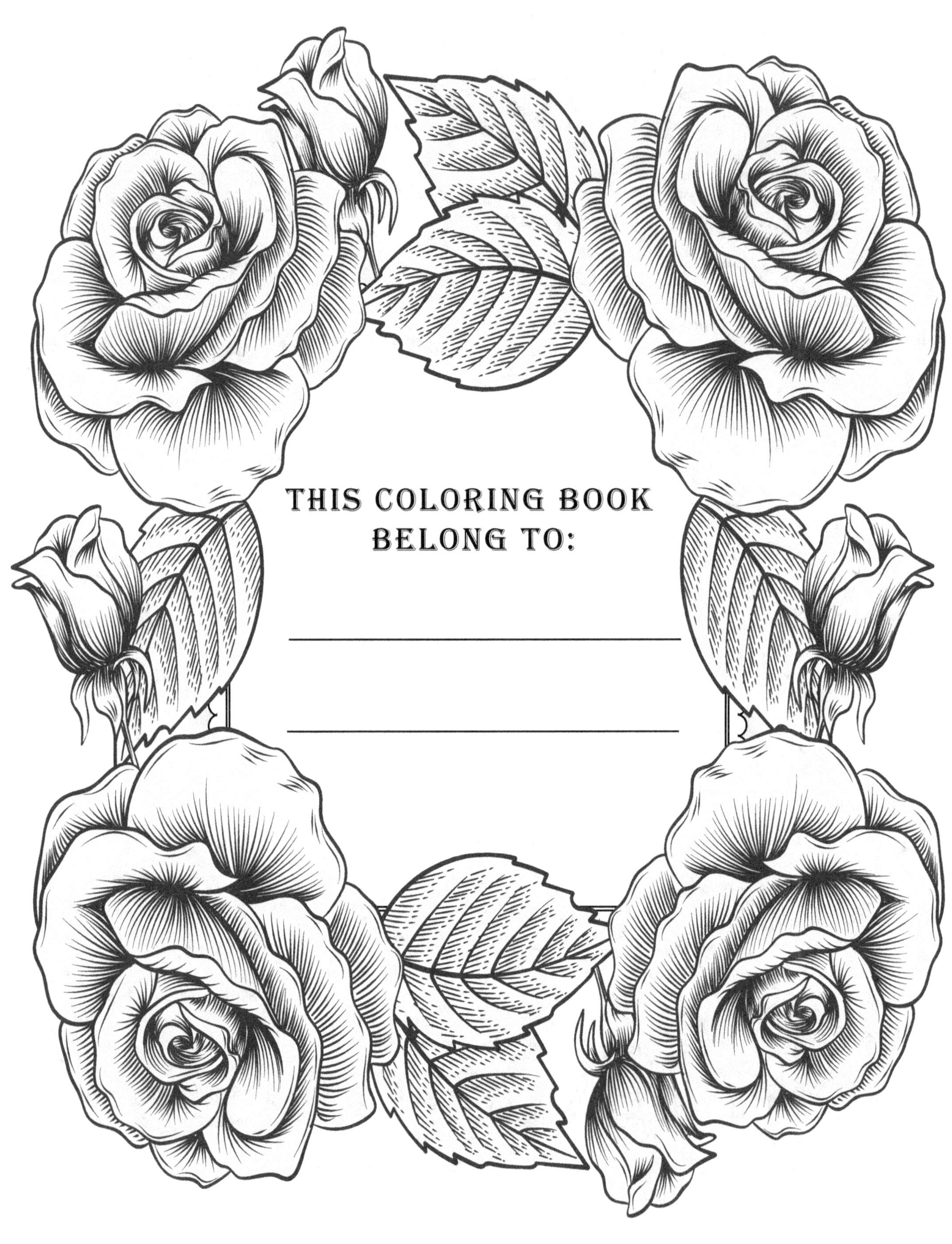

THIS COLORING BOOK
BELONG TO:

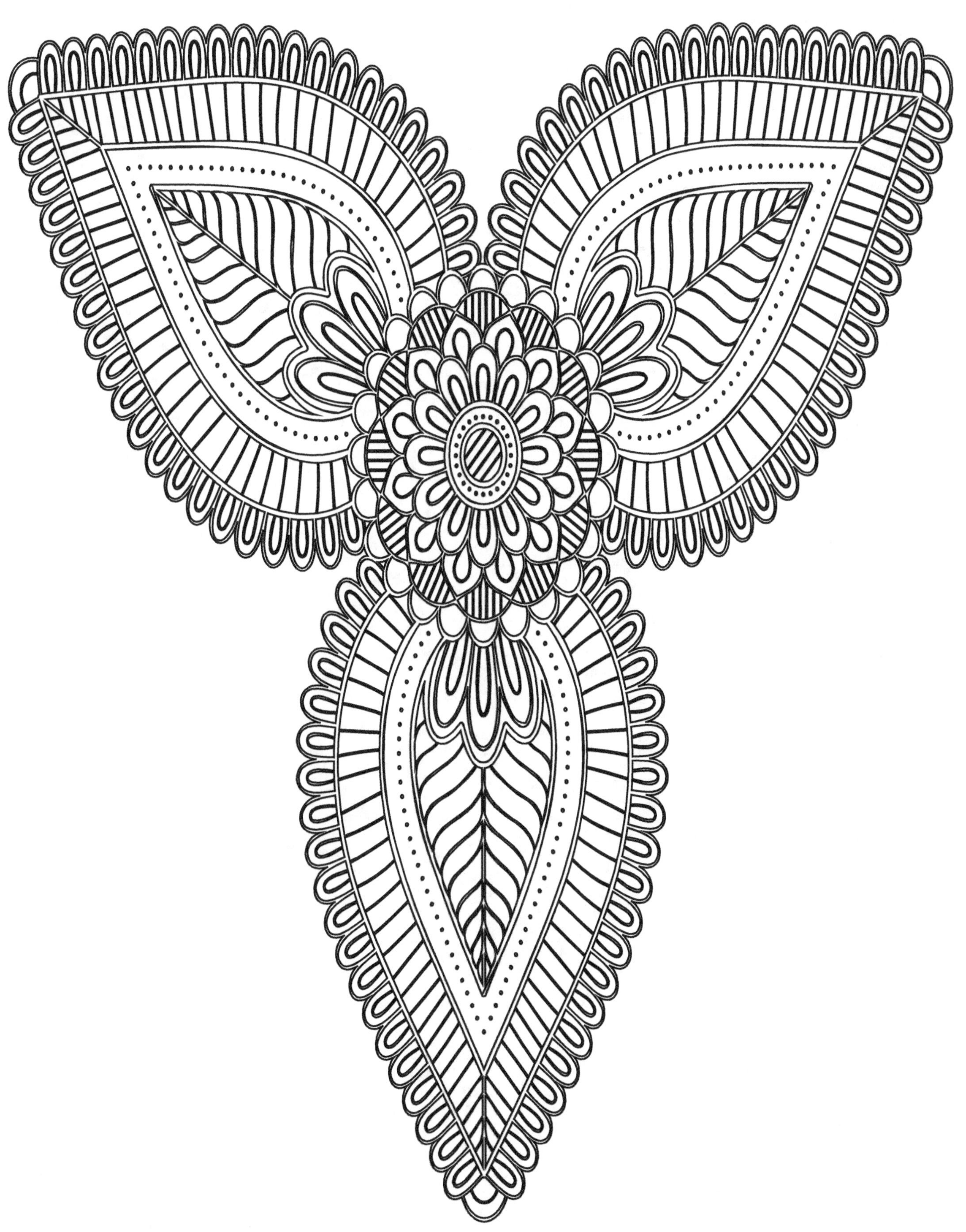

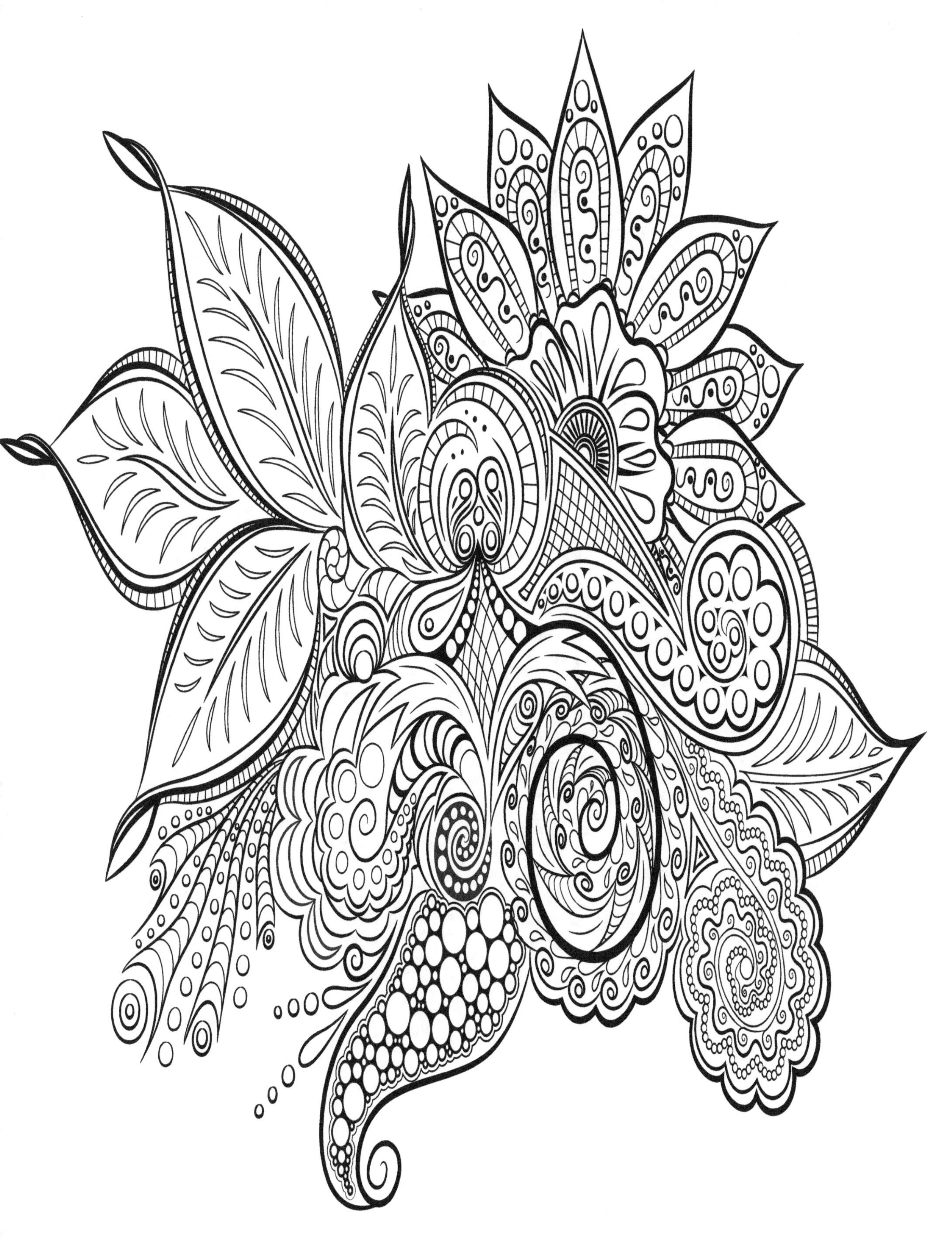

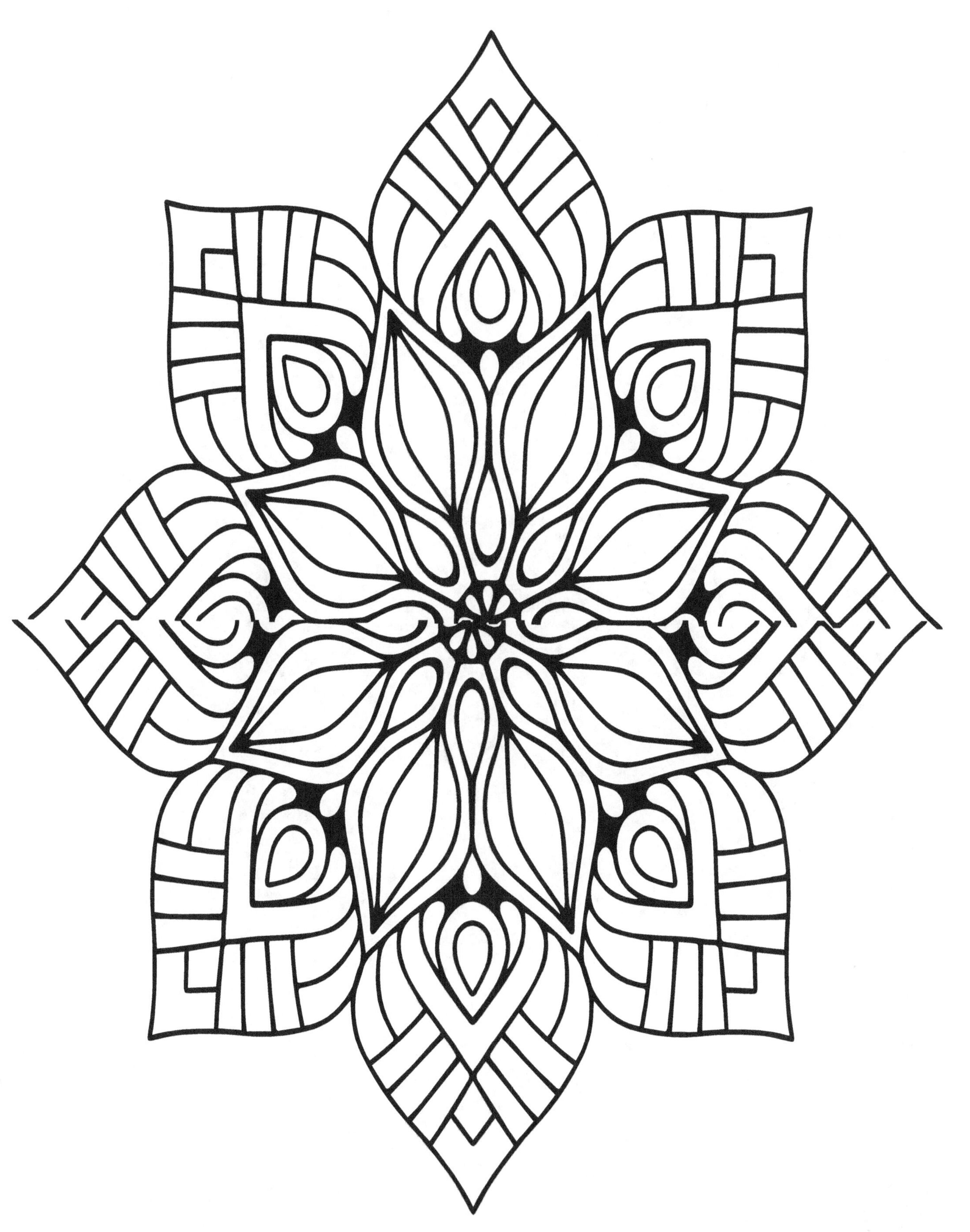

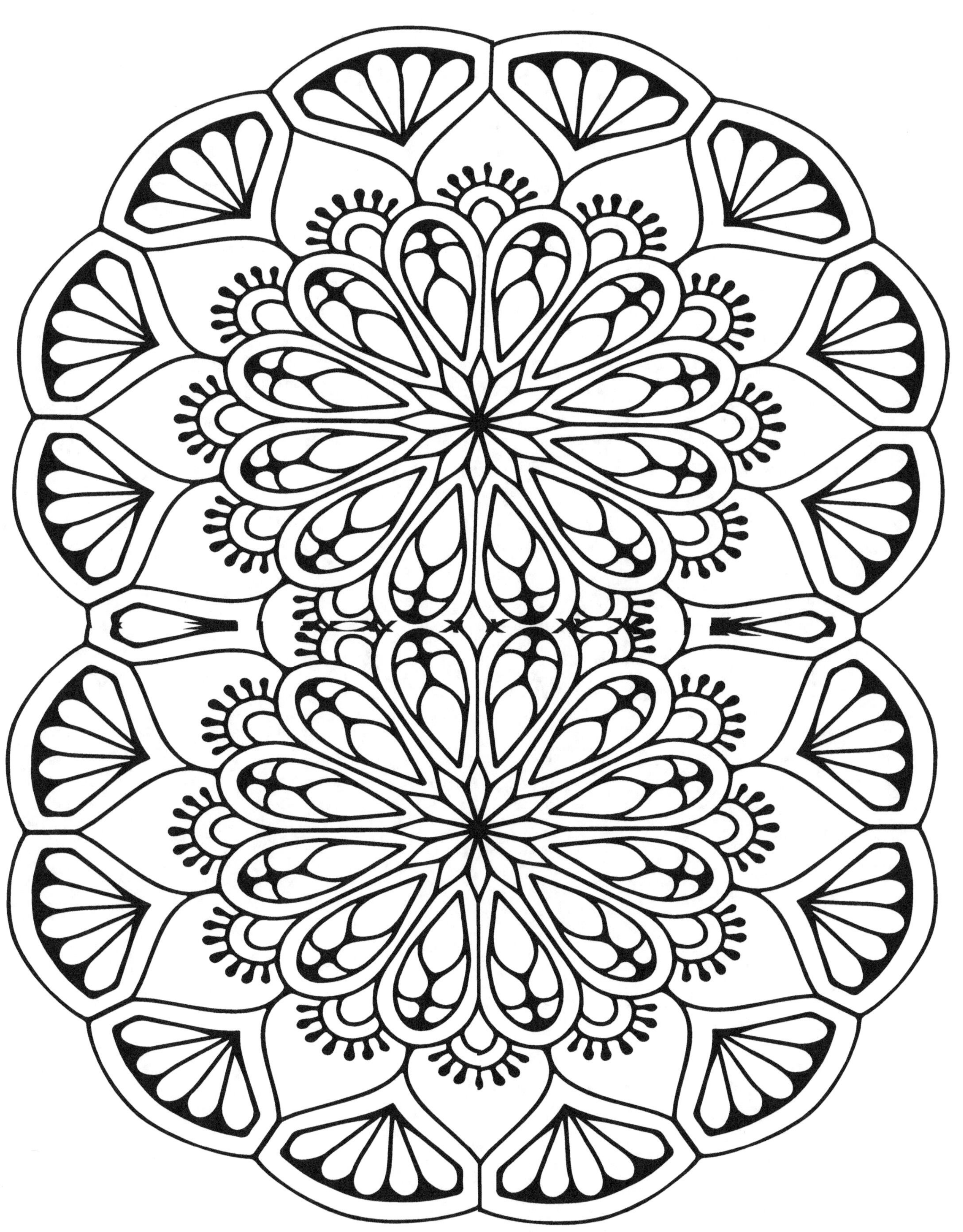

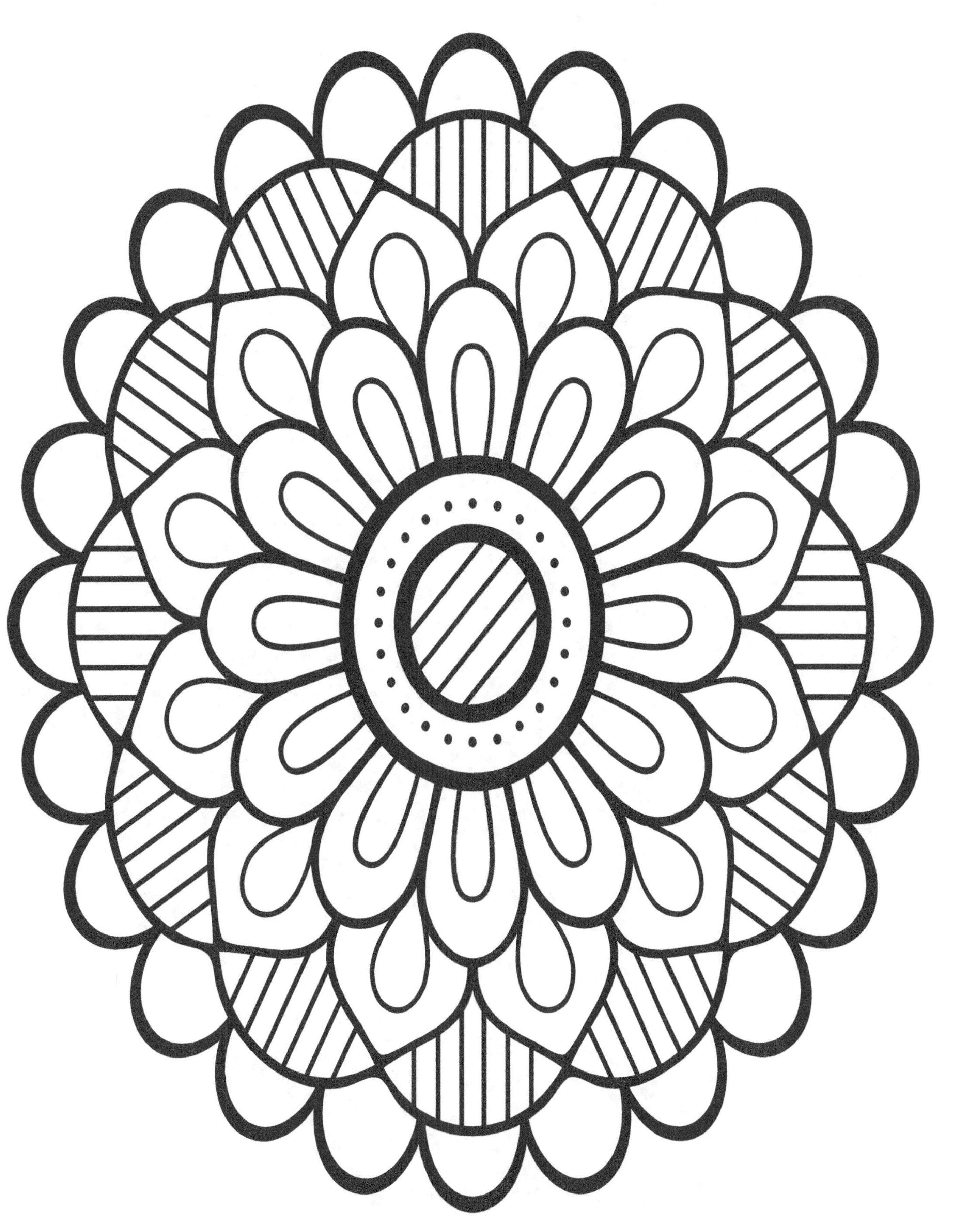

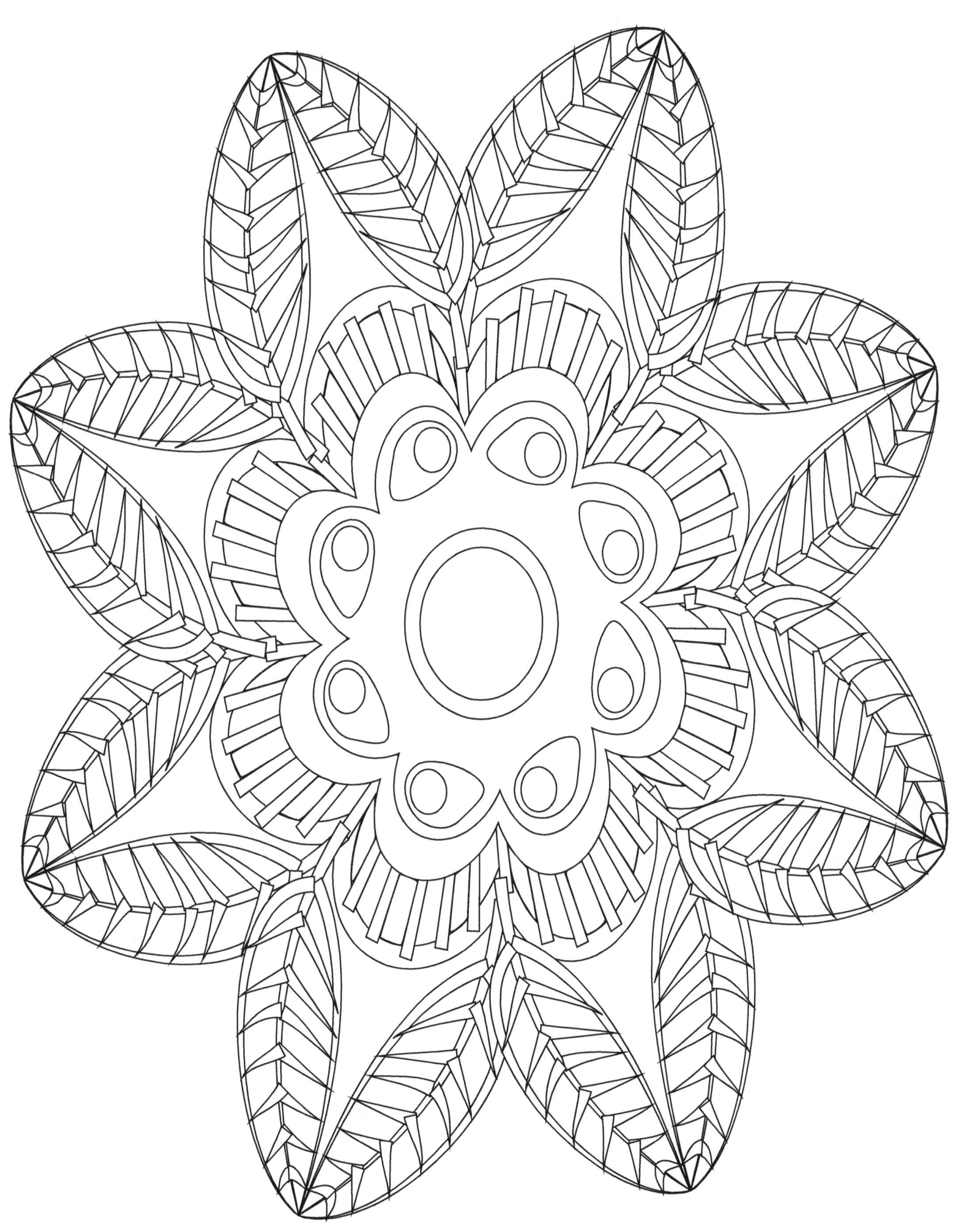

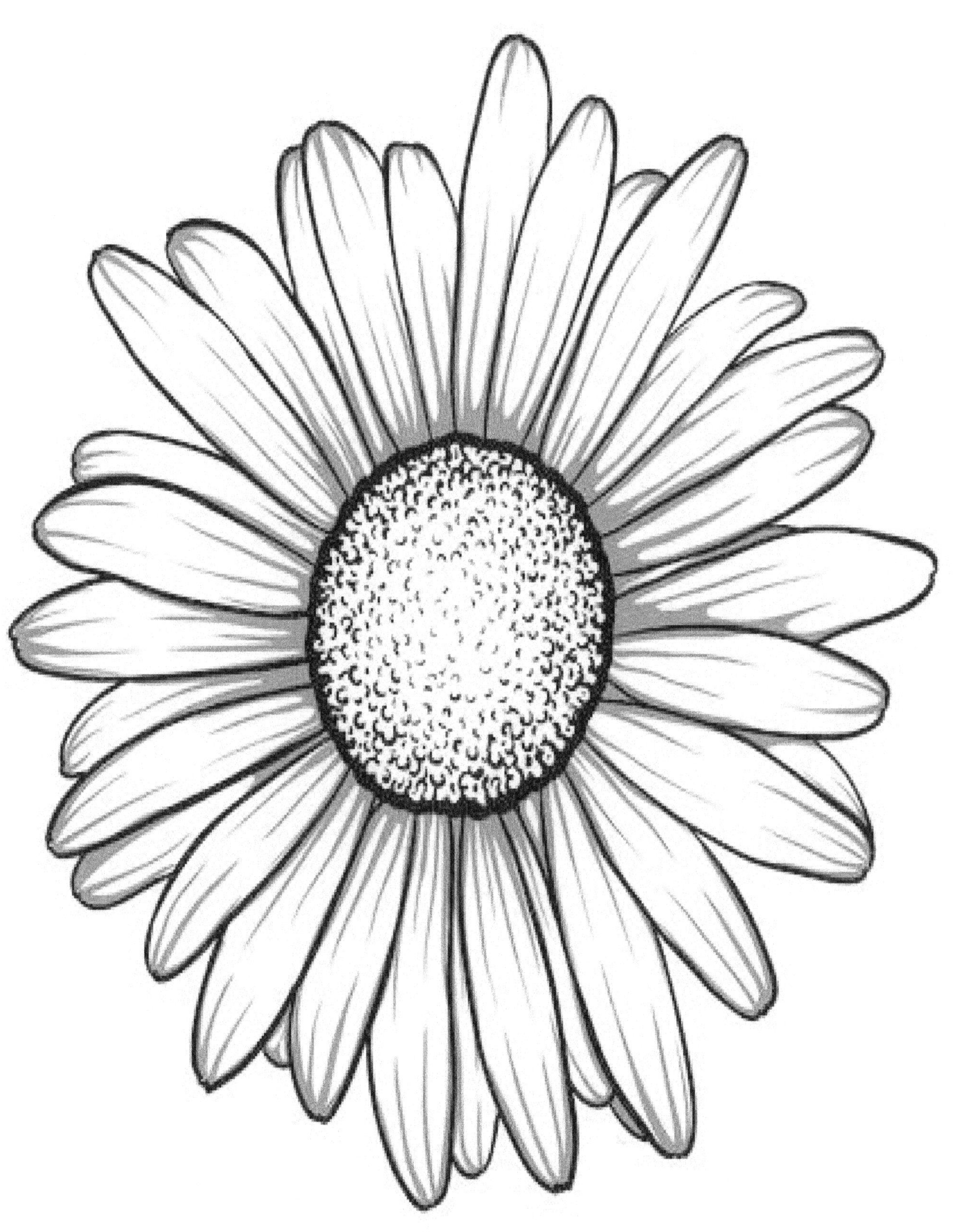

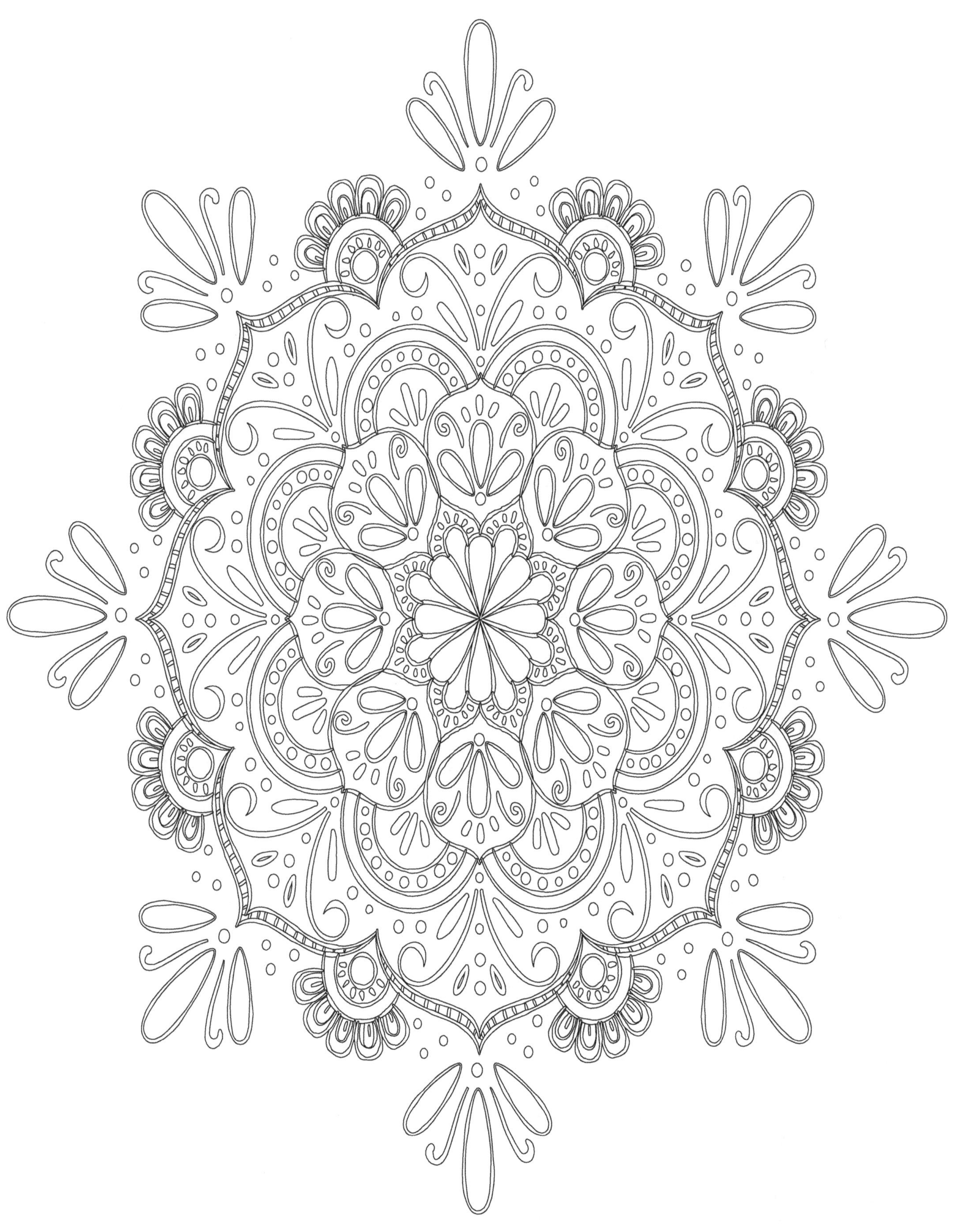

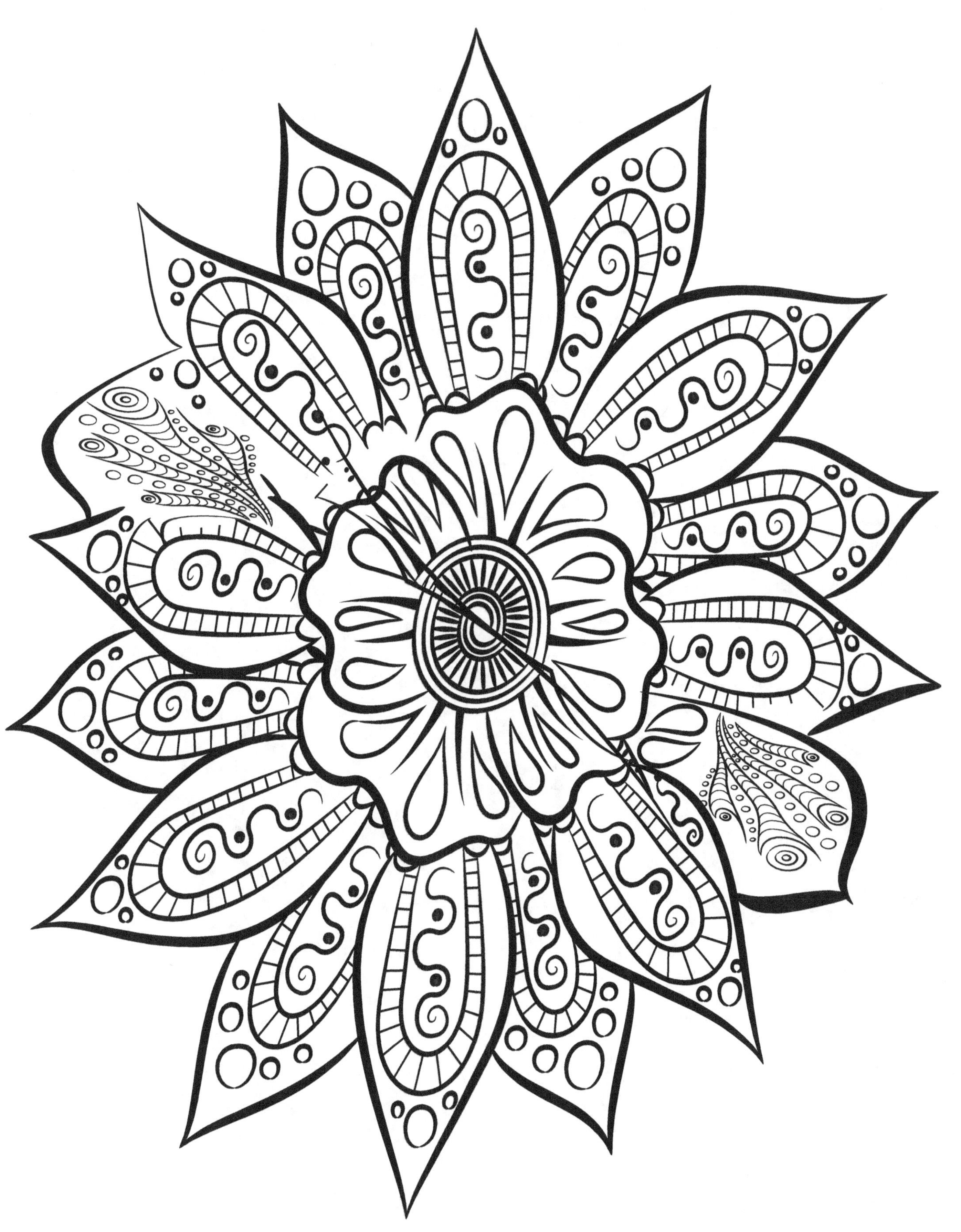

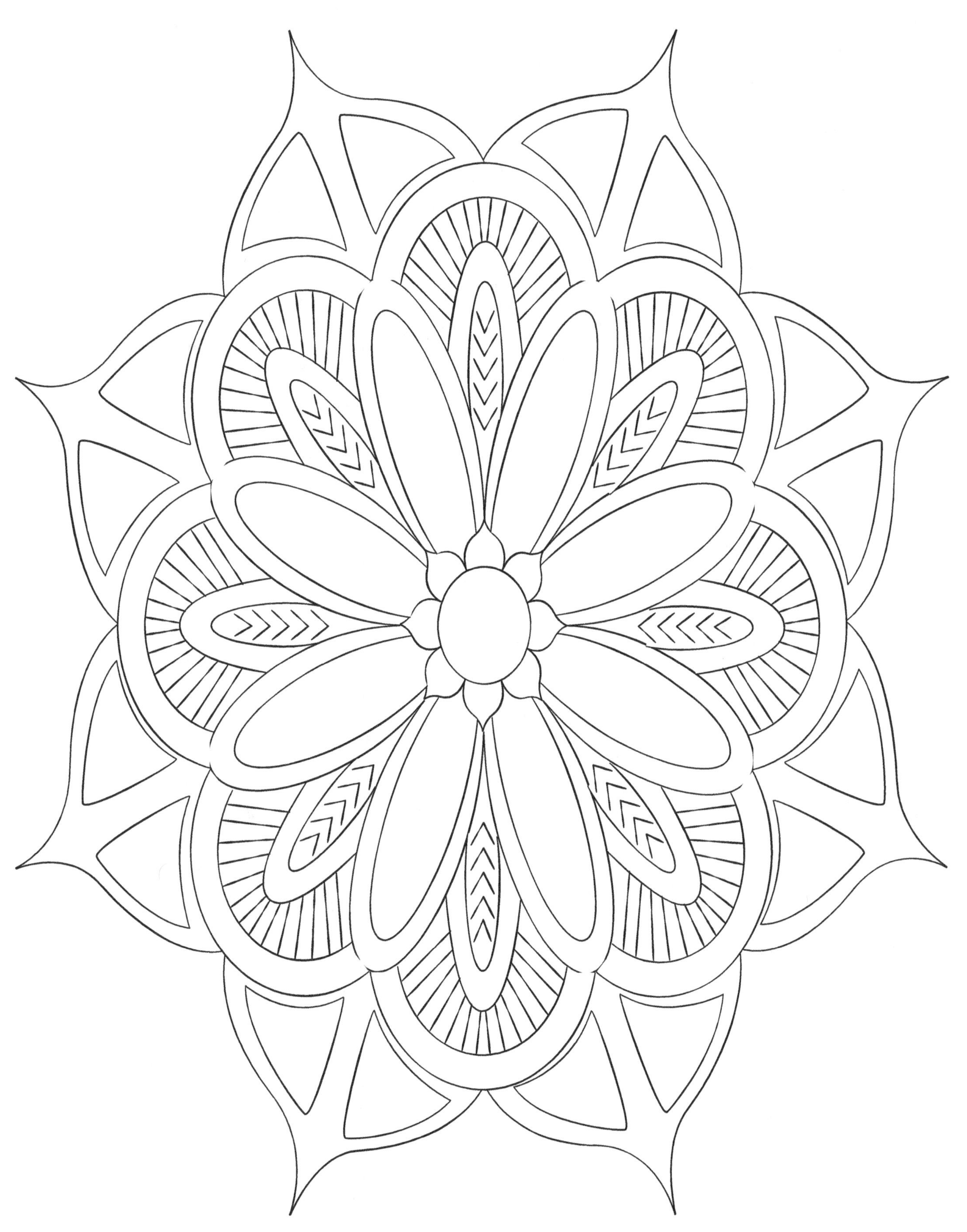

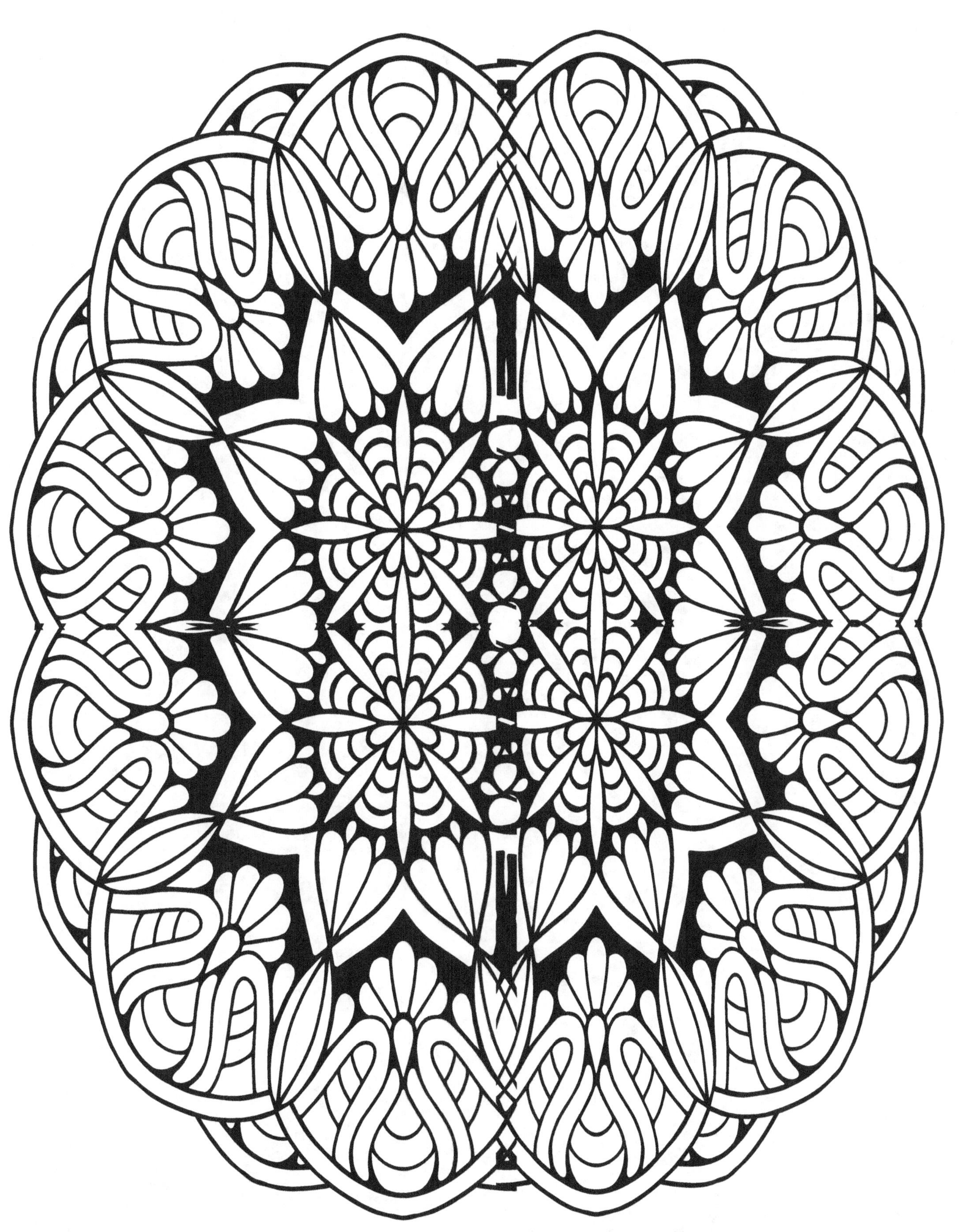

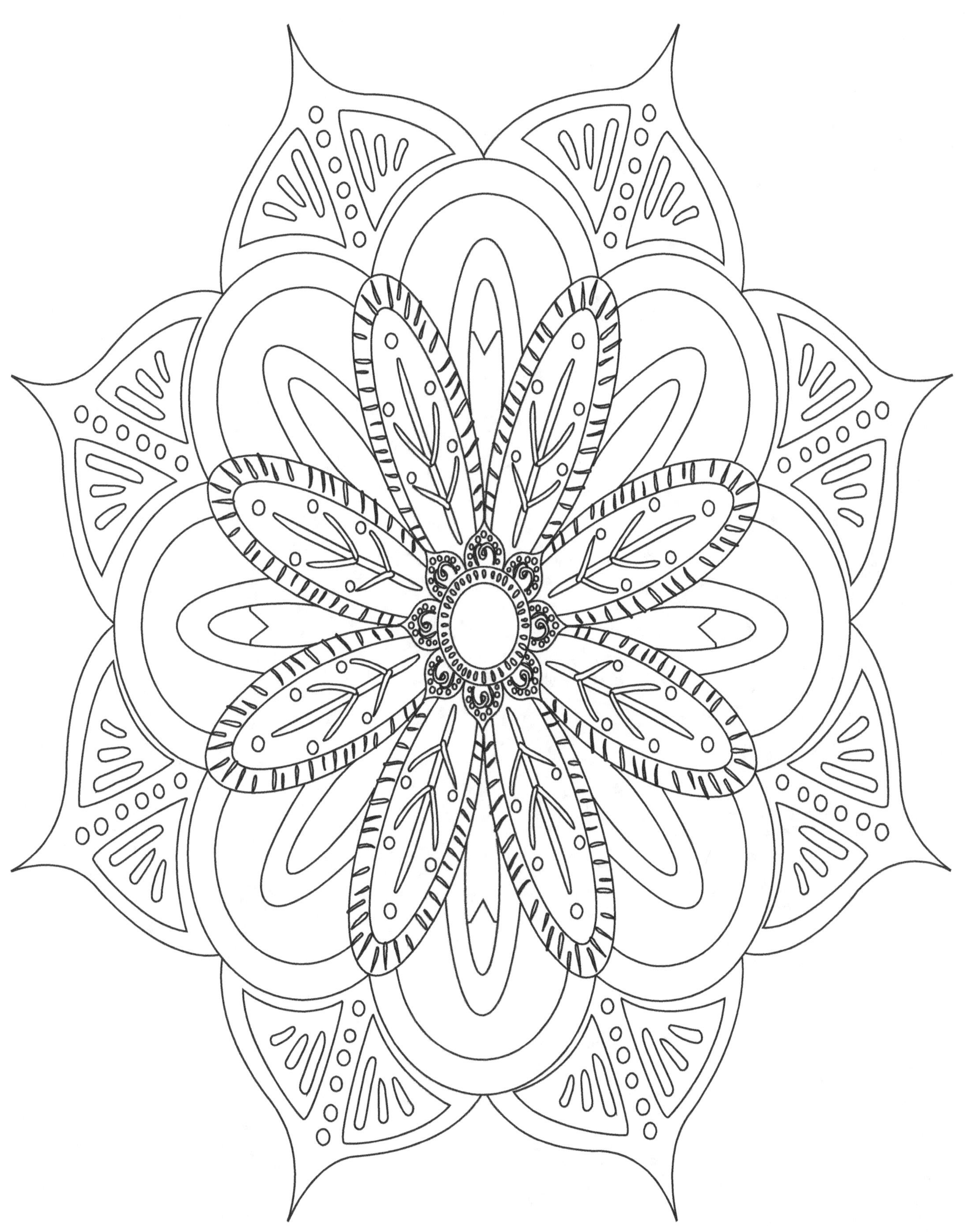

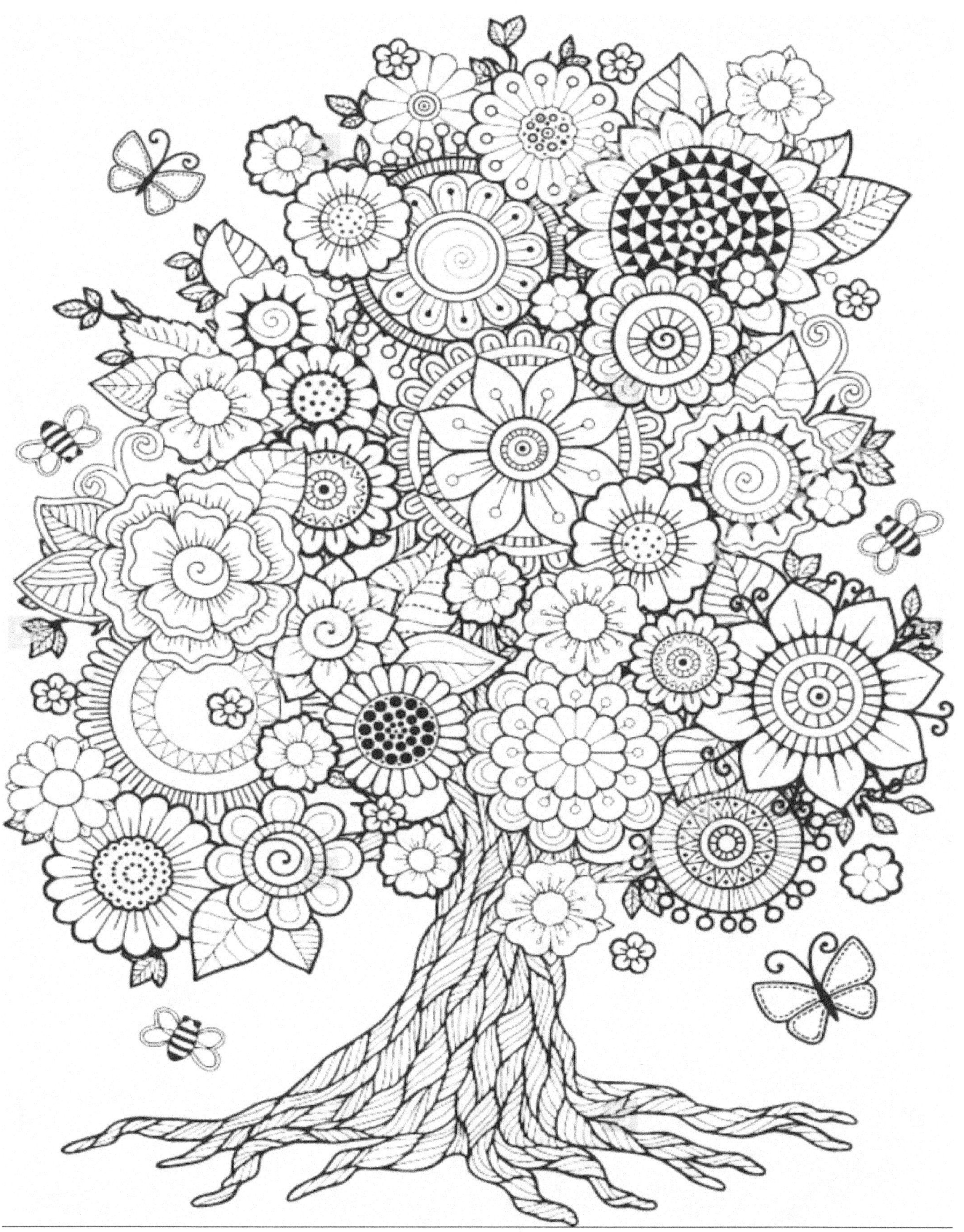

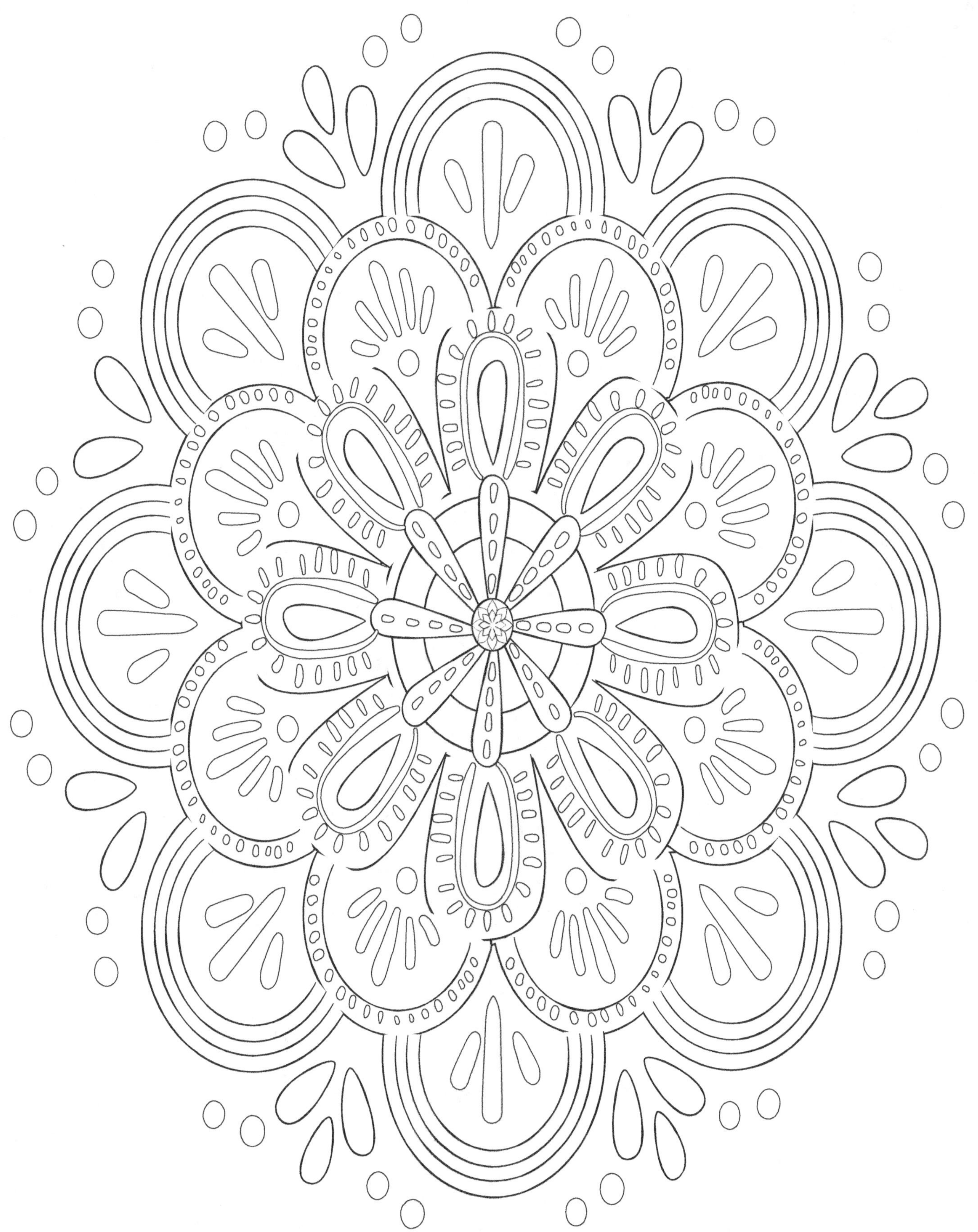

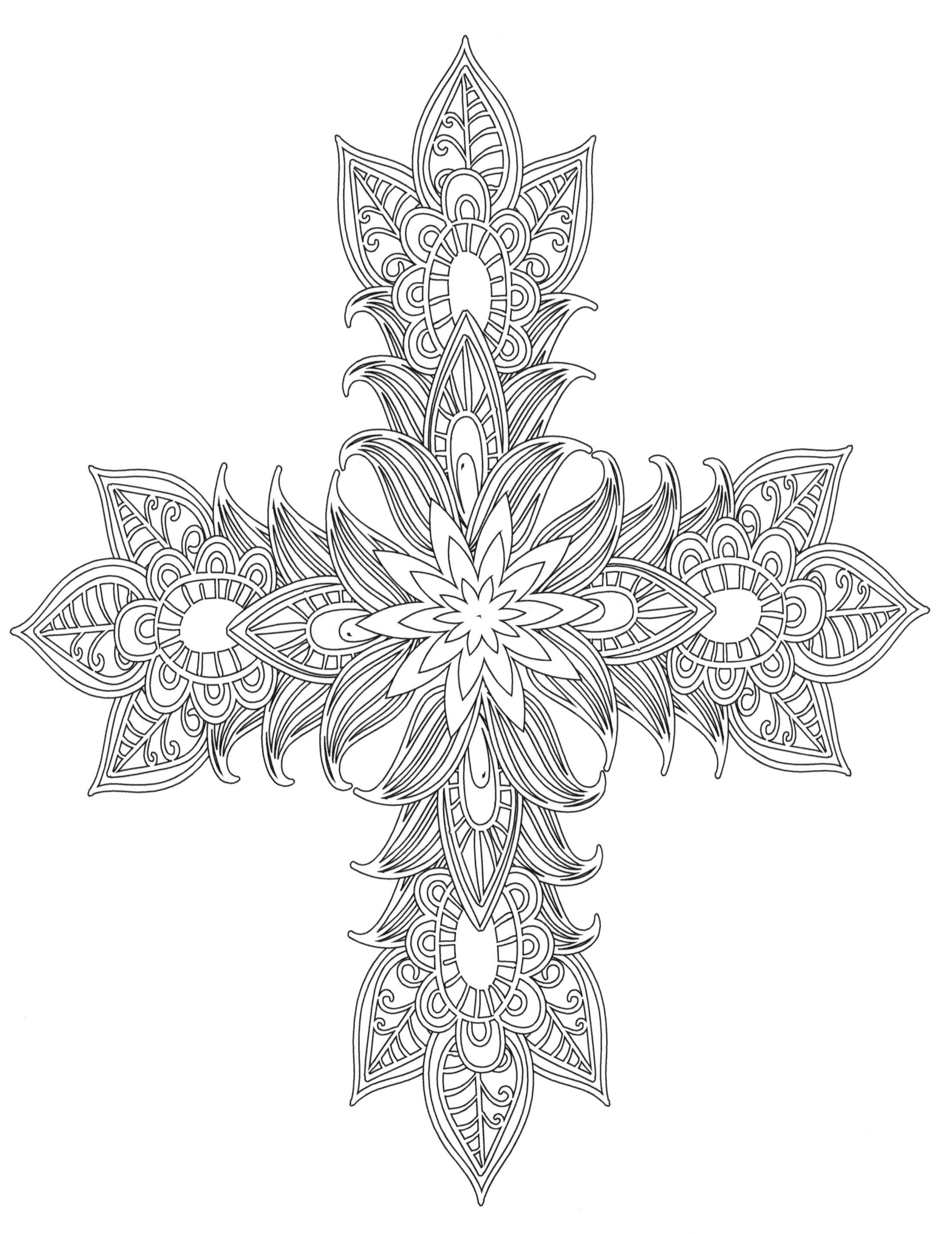

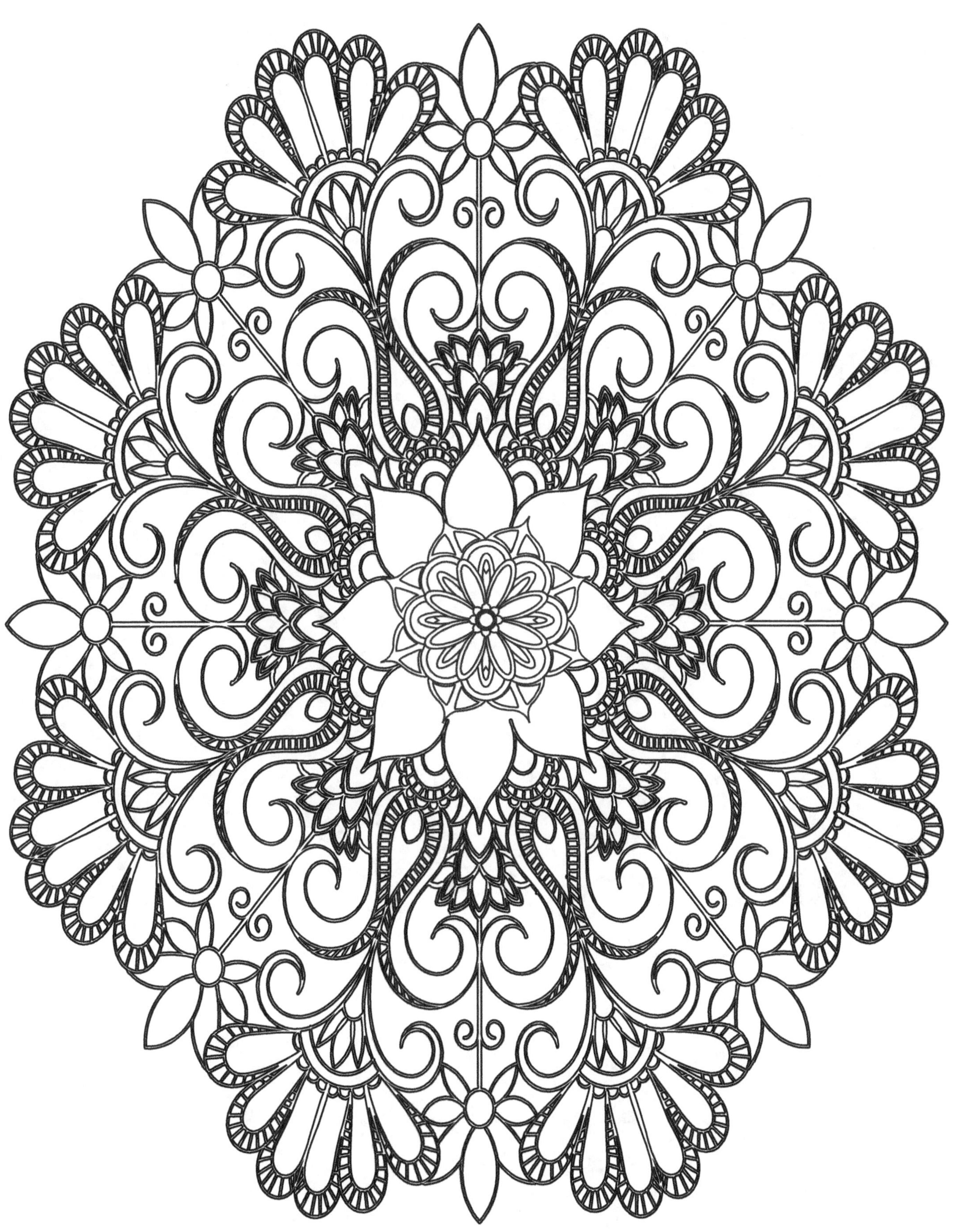

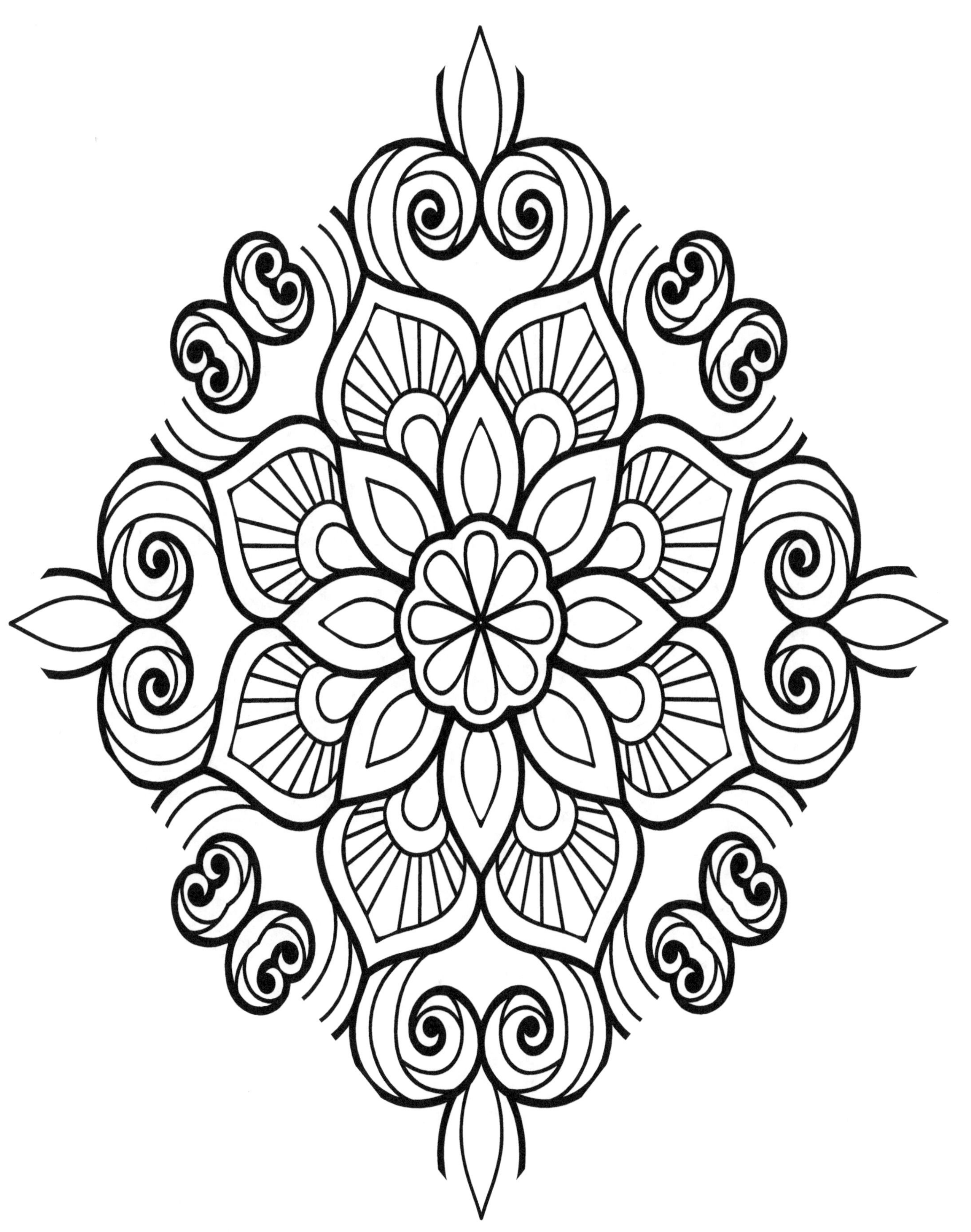

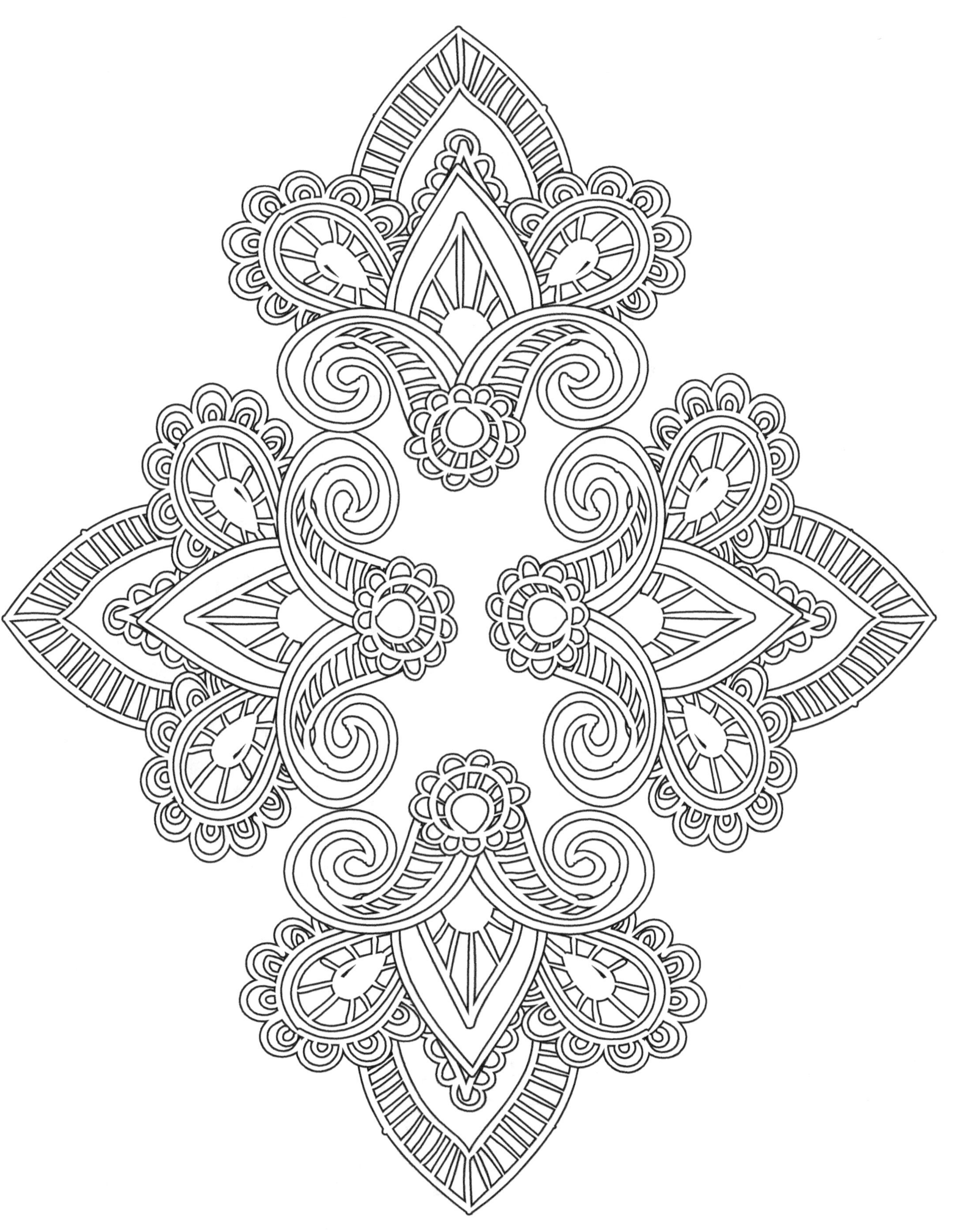

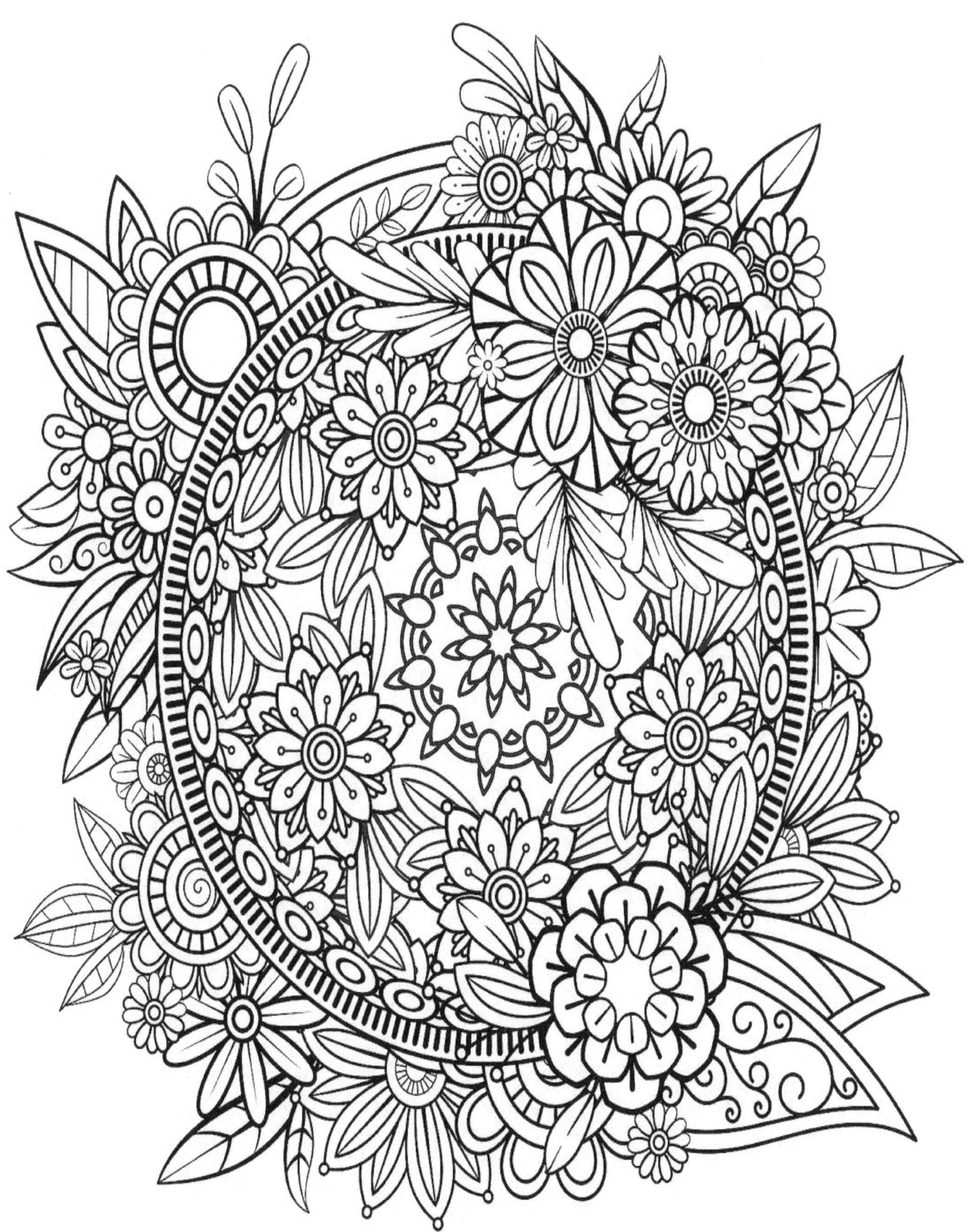

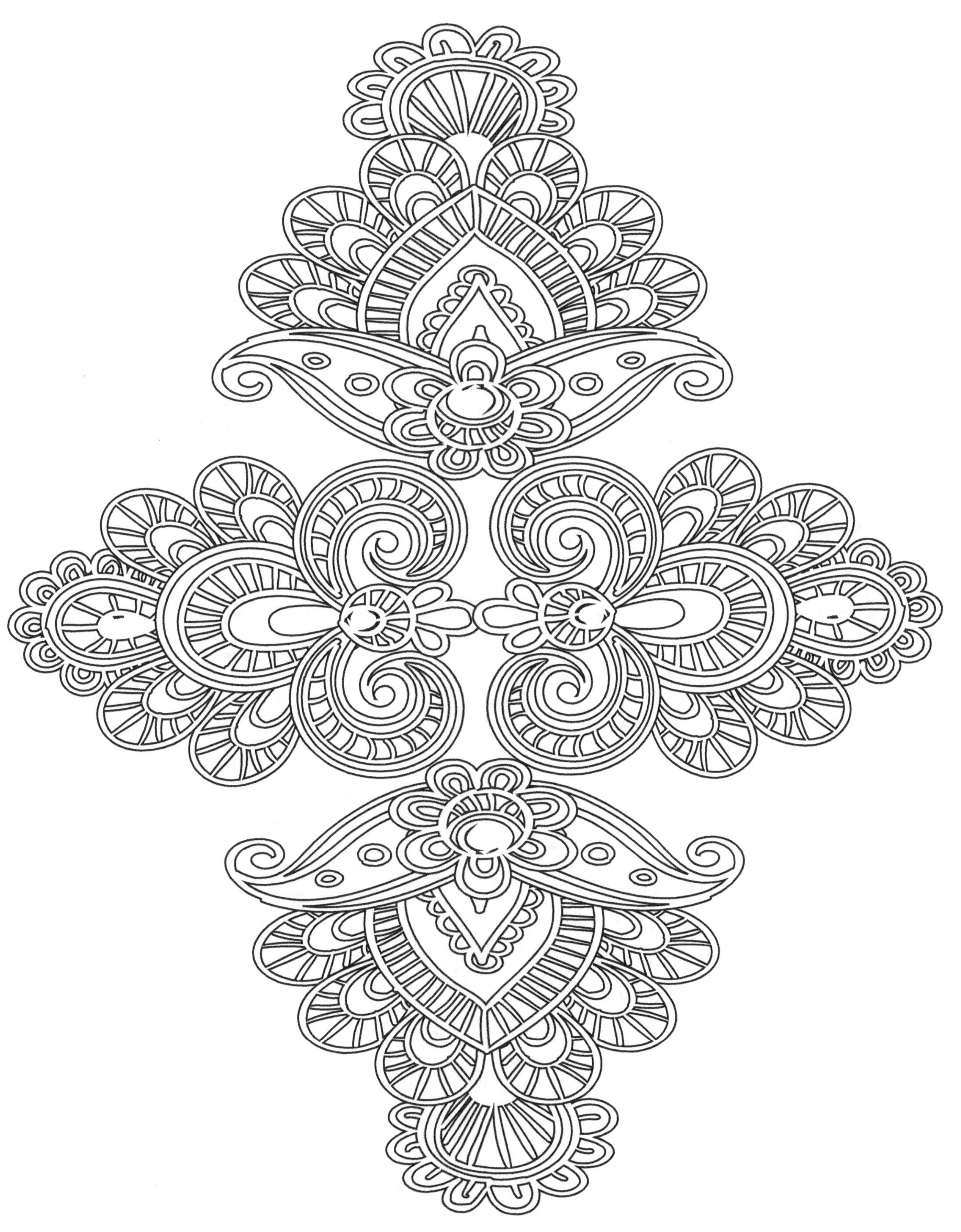

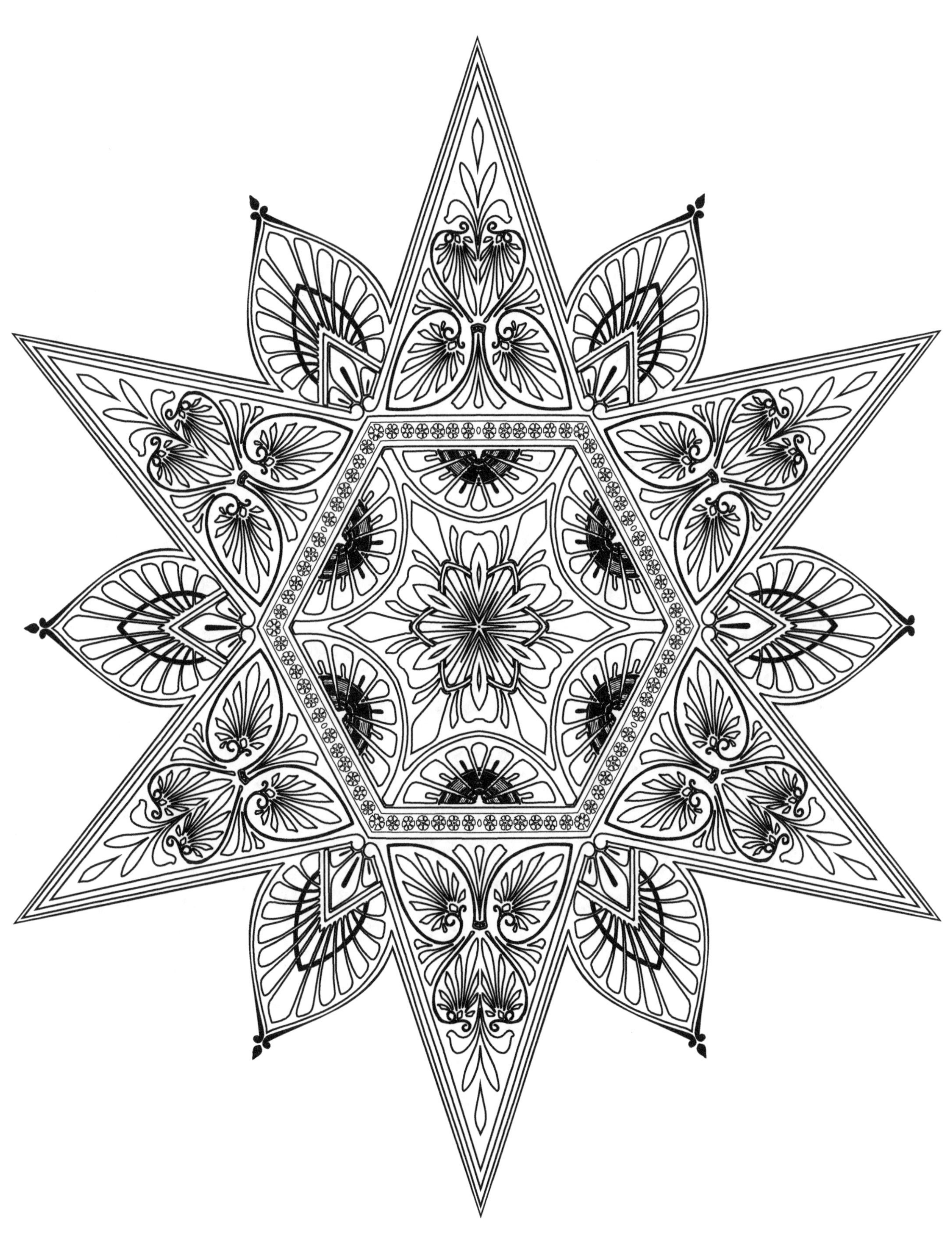

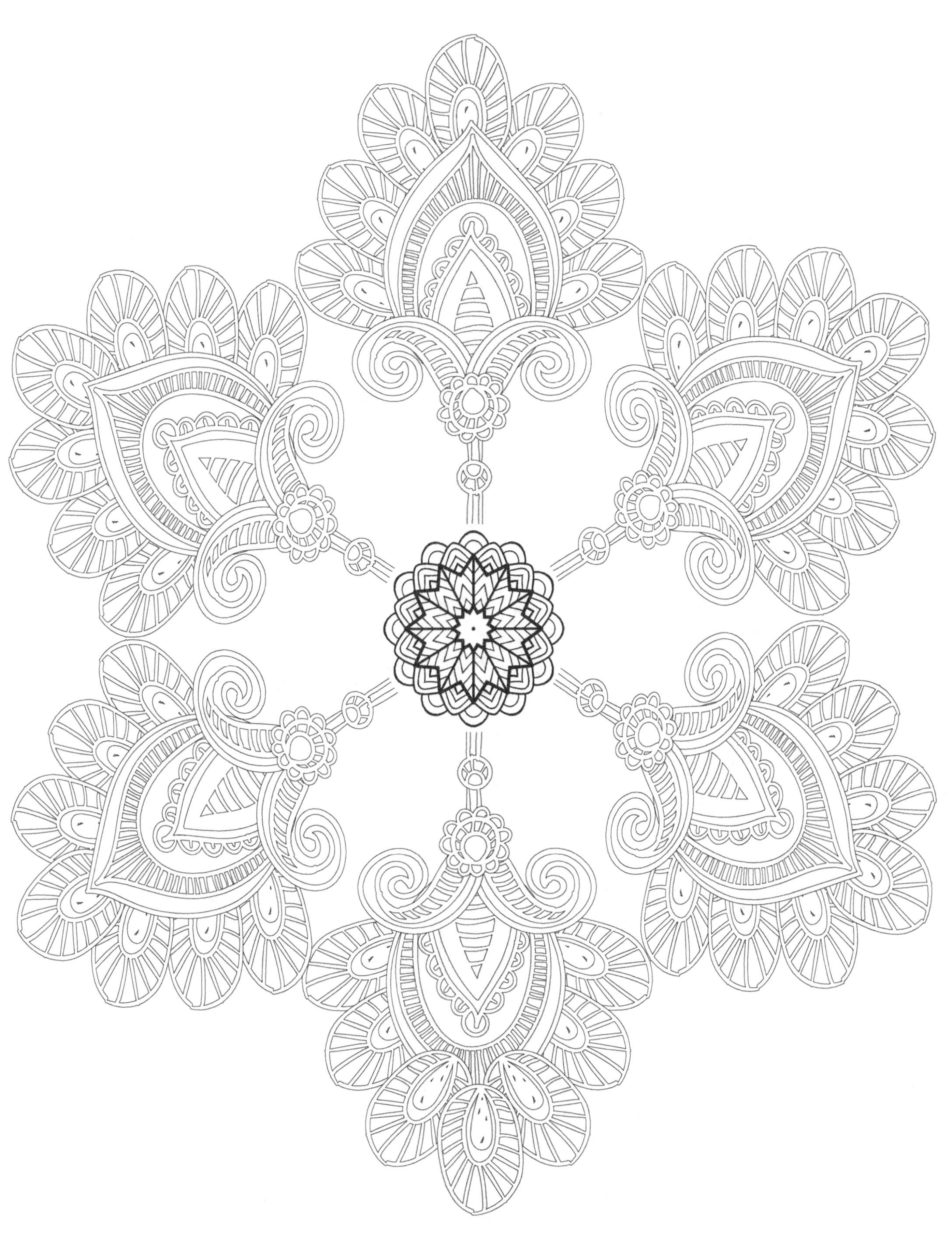

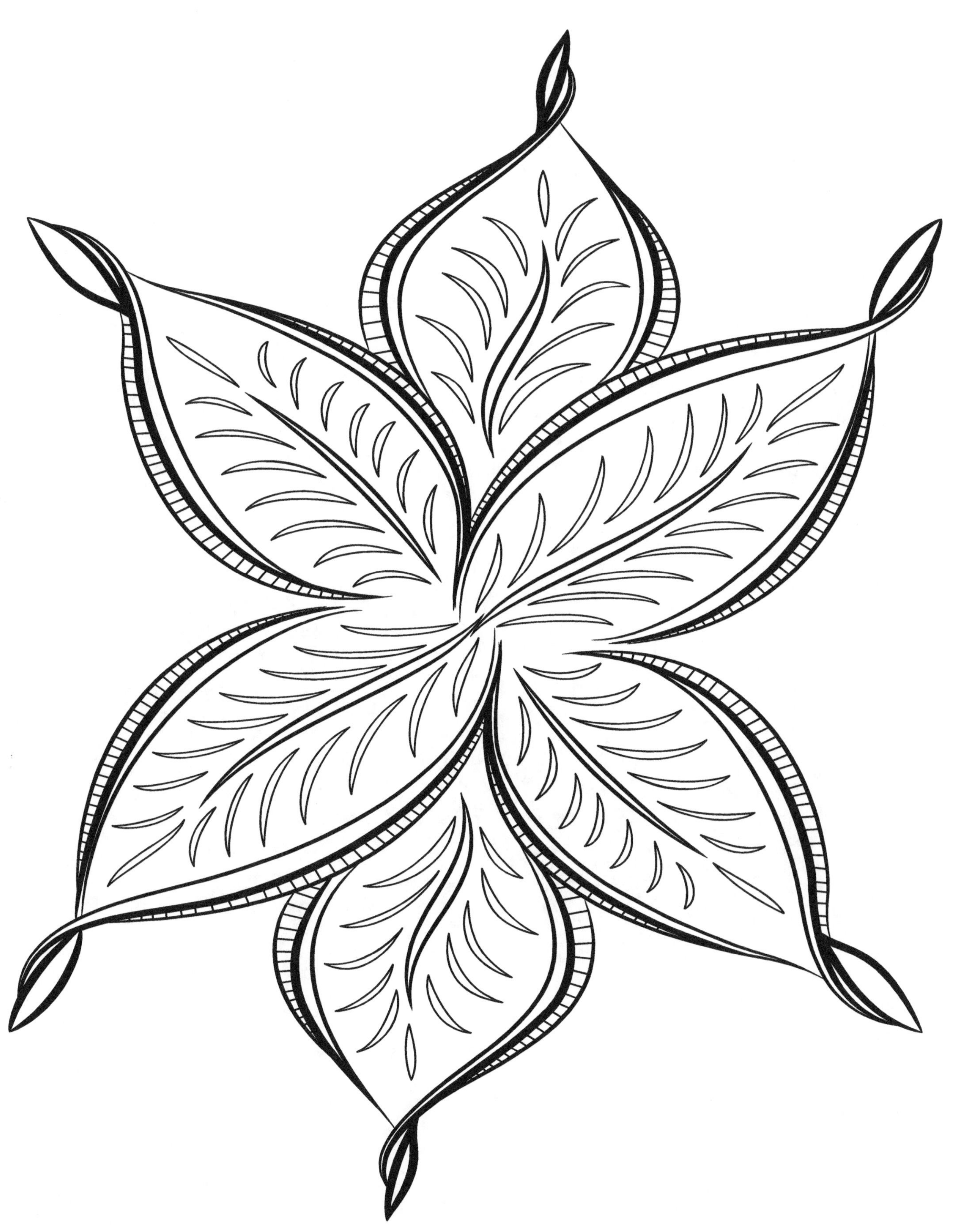

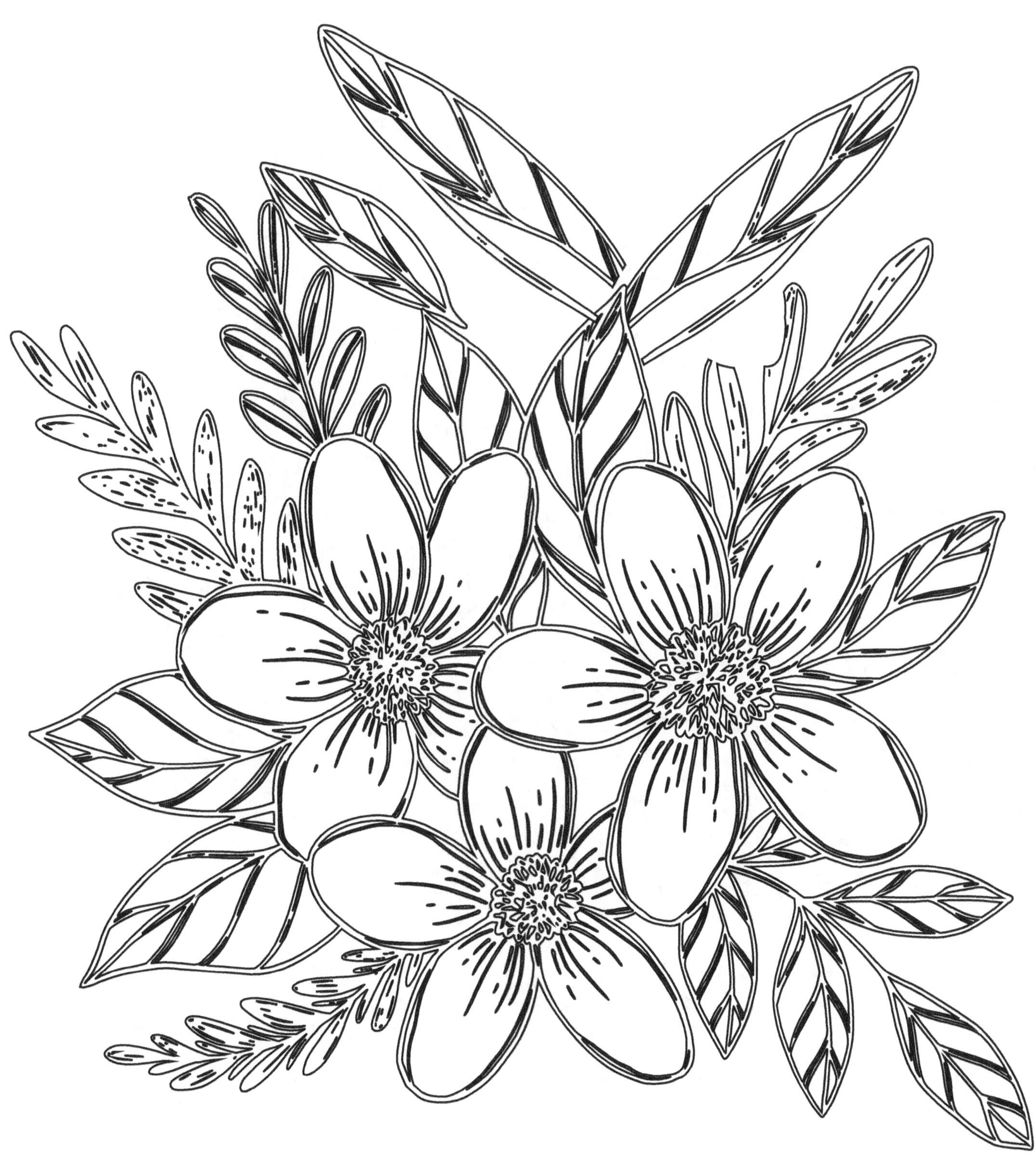

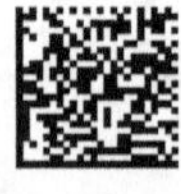